THE
Skinny
ICE CREAM
MAKER

CookNation

The Skinny Ice Cream Maker
Delicious Lower Fat, Lower Calorie Ice Cream, Frozen Yogurt & Sorbet Recipes For Your Ice Cream Maker

A Bell & Mackenzie Publication
First published in 2014 by Bell & Mackenzie Publishing
Limited.

ISBN 978-1-909855-49-6

A CIP catalogue record of this book is available from the
British Library

Disclaimer
This book is designed to provide information on the
dishes that can be cooked in an electric ice cream maker
appliance. However all devices vary so please ensure you
follow the cooking guidelines and instructions for your
individual device.
Some recipes may contain nuts or traces of nuts. Those
suffering from any allergies associated with nuts should
avoid any recipes containing nuts or nut based oils.
This information is provided and sold with the knowledge
that the publisher and author do not offer any legal or
other professional advice.
In the case of a need for any such expertise consult with
the appropriate professional.
This book does not contain all information available on the

Contents

Contents

Introduction

Introduction

Ice Cream can be the most delightful, exciting, fun and rewarding treat for anyone, young or old. It evokes and stimulates our memories of long hot summer days and makes our taste buds scream for more. From soft and creamy classics, indulgent and rich ripples to daring, exotic and delectable concoctions, ice cream is the king of treats.

With domestic ice cream makers now established as reliable and affordable, making your own ice cream at home couldn't be easier. Recreating your favourite iced treat is simple and quick and will rival any shop-bought equivalent! By following our simple recipes and ingredients you can be making delicious lower fat, lower calorie 'skinny' ice cream in no time....you'll never want to buy a store tub of ice cream again!

Making ice cream at home can be more expensive than buying from a supermarket but the rewards in taste and texture far outweigh the difference in cost, plus your ice cream will be free from the additional preservatives and emulsifiers that commercial ice creams contain to prolong their shelf life. You can experiment with flavours and textures and make quantities to suit you and your family. Best of all: every recipe in this book uses a lower fat alternative in the ingredients without compromising on taste or texture meaning you can reward yourself with a delicious guilt-free homemade treat in as little as 15 mins.

Our Skinny Ice Cream

Ice cream is often seen as an indulgence – something naughty but nice that we shouldn't allow ourselves to eat too often. While this is true to a certain extent, with our skinny recipes you can allow yourself these iced treats perhaps a little more often that you might normally do!

Our skinny ice cream, frozen yogurt and sorbet recipes are all lower in fat, calories and sugar than the many traditional full fat shop-bought products or other recipes you may research. By replacing the ingredients with some key alternatives you can spoil yourself with a reduced fat/calorie/sugar delight.

The key alternative ingredients we have used throughout the recipe book are as follows:

• Low fat yogurt
• Silver Spoon 'Half Spoon' Sugar/Splenda Sugar Blend
• Skimmed milk
• Low fat crème fraiche
• Low fat custard
• Light condensed milk

Don't be tempted to add additional ingredients or toppings if you are watching your weight. Even ingredients such as dried fruit and nuts can dramatically increase calories. That said, experimenting and creating your own recipes can be very rewarding.

Frozen Yogurts

Frozen yogurts, iced yogurts or 'fro-yo's' as they are also known have become a multi million dollar industry in their own right in recent years. Originally intended as an alternative to ice cream frozen yogurts tend to be more tart in taste and lower in fat than regular ice cream. Frozen yogurts should be consumed ideally same day but can be kept in the freezer for a few days. If you do store in the freezer, allow the yogurt to soften up in a refrigerator for 30-40 minutes before serving.

It is worth noting that our 'skinny' frozen yogurts, as with our ice cream and sorbets are not intended as a replacement for a meal if your are on a diet or a weight management plan. Although lower in fat, calories and sugar, the toppings that play a big part in commercial iced yogurts can increase these elements dramatically. Stick to natural fruit toppings where possible.

Sorbets

A sorbet is a light frozen dessert, which usually contains no dairy such as cream, yogurt, milk, custard or eggs. Typically it is made with pureed fruit or fruit juice with an added sweetener. Excellent sorbets can be made with an ice cream maker. Consistency should be slightly slushy. If you are freezing your sorbets, allow the to soften in a refrigerator for about 30 minutes before serving.

About ice Cream Makers

Domestic ice cream makers are now commonplace. There are many different models on the market ranging in price from £15 ($25) to £250 ($420) with professional models starting at £2000 ($3365)! As with all investments, your budget will dictate which type of ice cream maker you choose. There are some very good budget ice cream makers available which will make excellent ice cream, so spending more money doesn't always mean better results. However as with all electrical/ mechanical appliances, the more expensive machines tend to use higher quality components, which over time may last longer than a cheaper model. You should select your model carefully based on price, customer reviews, capacity, ease of use and manufacturers guarantees & customer service.

To follow is a general guide to the 2 main types of ice cream maker currently on the market and how they work. You should of course study the manufacturers guidelines and instructions for your own model before use.

Built-in Freezer Ice Cream Maker

These machines have a built in freezer so there is no need to pre-freeze a bowl in the freezer before making your ice cream. It works by churning and freezing simultaneously, making ice cream from scratch in as little as 20 minutes. It will also keep your ice cream cool for up to 10 mins once churning has completed.

The machine when switched on will rapidly bring the bowl to the required temperature for making ice cream then all you need to do is switch on the paddle and add your ingredients.

Ice cream makers with a built in freezer can offer a larger capacity, but not always, so do your research before purchasing. The major advantage of this type of appliance is its ability to make different batches of ice cream one after the other. The built in freezing feature means all you need to do is clean the inner bowl then wait a few minutes for it to refreeze before starting again. No pre-planning needed. Excellent texture can also be achieved with this type of machine. If counter space is an issue you should be aware that built in freezer models tend to be larger in size and heavier than those that have a removable bowl for freezing. Built in freezing also makes this appliance more expensive.

Pre-Freeze Ice Cream Maker

These are perhaps the most popular ice cream makes as they are more affordable. Unlike the built-in freezer models they require the churning bowl to be pre-frozen for a minimum of 8-12 hours in a freezer before use and therefore the cost is dramatically lower. This requires pre-planning before you can make your ice cream although you can purchase additional bowls so one can always be kept in the freezer ready to use.

The electric paddle is housed in the lid of the model and attaches to the churning bowl. Generally, smaller quantities of ice cream can be made using this type of machine and some models are less successful at preventing large ice particles forming which in turn can affect texture. Researching your model and reading customer reviews should satisfy you to this extent.

Price is the major advantage with this model although pre-freezing the bowl doesn't suit everyone.

Budget will no doubt dictate which model you choose but excellent results can be achieved in both types of machines.

Tips
• All the recipes in The Skinny Ice Cream Maker are simple, easy and produce great results. We've put together some helpful tips and tricks which should help you make the most of your ice cream maker and our recipes.

• Pre-freeze your bowl according to the manufacturers instructions. Most will advise 24 hours but some can be as little as 8 hours. Don't be tempted to freeze for less as this will affect the quality of your ice cream. Best practice is to always keep your bowl in the freezer ready to use.
• Wrap your bowl in a plastic bag before freezing. This will prevent freezer burn and ice crystals building up.

• Keep ingredients refrigerated prior to use where applicable.

• Use the freshest ingredients available and those in 'season' for the best flavour.

• Additional ingredients such as nuts, dried fruit and chocolate chips should only be added at the last minute to evenly distribute them.

• All recipes are best eaten immediately, however if you do wish to freeze them, store your ice cream, yogurts or sorbets in flat plastic containers in the freezer. This will allow for more even consistency.

• To prevent ice crystals forming on the top of ice cream place a layer of cling film or grease proof paper over the top before putting on the lid.

• Don't store your ice cream for too long. It will lose some of its flavour and texture over time and the lack of preservatives present in shop bought ice cream means it's best to eat as quickly as possible – ideally within a week or two weeks maximum.

• Do not refreeze ice cream that has thawed as this will pose a risk of bacteria growing.

• Thoroughly clean your ice cream maker after each batch using boiling water to sterilize.

• Make half quantities if this suits you better. All our recipes should make 8-10 scoops but you can reduce the quantities easily to make less. Our scoop size is based on a 40g serving.

• Do not overfill the bowl. Three quarters full should be the maximum to allow air to get into the mixture.

• After churning is complete, transfer your ice cream to the freezer for 2-3 hours to firm up.

• To serve ice cream that has been frozen, remove from the freezer 10 minutes before serving or to the refrigerator for 30 minutes.

• To scoop ice cream perfectly from the container use a spring loaded scoop or strong metal dessert spoon dipped in warm water.

Skinny ice cream

Helpful Tips

Remember if you are freezing your ice cream, remove from the freezer approx. 10-15 minutes before serving or to the refrigerator for approx. 30-35 minutes to get the best serving texture.

Skinny ice cream

Simple Strawberry Ice Cream

Ingredients

- 400g/14oz fresh strawberries
- 40g/1½oz Silver Spoon 'Half Spoon' Sugar or Splenda Sugar Blend
- 200ml/7floz low fat crème fraiche
- 1 tsp lemon juice

Method

- First blend the strawberries into a puree.
- Add the sugar, crème fraiche & lemon juice and gently combine.
- Cover and leave to chill for 20-30 minutes.
- Add to the ice cream maker to churn and freeze according to your device instructions.
- Eat and enjoy immediately, or place in a container and store in the freezer.

55 cals per scoop

If you want the ice cream to have a completely smooth texture sieve the strawberry puree to remove the seeds, before adding the other ingredients.

Light Chocolate Ice Cream

Ingredients

- 50g/2oz milk chocolate, melted
- 15g/½oz Silver Spoon 'Half Spoon' Sugar or Splenda Sugar Blend
- 300ml/10floz low fat crème fraiche
- 200g/7oz low fat ready-made custard

Method

- Allow the melted chocolate to cool.
- Gently combine all the ingredients together.
- Cover and leave to chill for 20-30 minutes.
- Add to the ice cream maker to churn and freeze according to your device instructions.
- Eat and enjoy immediately, or place in a container and store in the freezer.

Use a good quality chocolate to get the best taste out of this ice cream.

68 cals per scoop

Lemon
Ice Cream

Ingredients

- 300ml/10floz light condensed milk
- 200ml/7floz low fat crème fraiche
- Juice of 2 lemons or 6 tbsp lemon juice

Method

- Gently combine all the ingredients together.
- Cover and leave to chill for 20-30 minutes.
- Add to the ice cream maker to churn and freeze according to your device instructions.
- Eat and enjoy immediately, or place in a container and store in the freezer.

77 cals
per scoop

Use fresh lemon juice if you can for this super-light tasting ice. Adjust the lemon quantity to suit your own taste.

Chocolate Chip Ice Cream

Ingredients

- 75g/3oz milk chocolate, melted
- 15g/½oz Silver Spoon 'Half Spoon' Sugar or Splenda Sugar Blend
- 200ml/7floz low fat crème fraiche
- 300g/10oz low fat ready-made custard
- 25g/1oz chocolate chips

Method

- Allow the melted chocolate to cool and gently combine with sugar, crème fraiche & custard.
- Cover and leave to chill for 20-30 minutes.
- Add to the ice cream maker to churn and freeze according to your device instructions.
- When the ice cream has reached the desired consistency tip in the chocolate chips and combine in the ice cream maker for a few seconds.
- Eat and enjoy immediately, or place in a container and store in the freezer.

Give the chocolate chips a bash with a rolling pin to crush them. It makes the chocolate go further and means you don't need to add as much.

82 cals
per scoop

Mandarin Orange & Dark Chocolate Ice Cream

Ingredients

- 75g/3oz dark chocolate, melted
- 200g/7oz tinned mandarin pieces, drained
- 200ml/7floz low fat crème fraiche
- 200g/7oz low fat ready-made custard

Method

- Allow the melted chocolate to cool for a few minutes.
- Blend the mandarin pieces into a puree.
- Gently combine the chocolate, mandarin pieces, crème fraiche & custard together.
- Cover and leave to chill for 20-30 minutes.
- Add to the ice cream maker to churn and freeze according to your device instructions.
- Eat and enjoy immediately, or place in a container and store in the freezer.

80 cals per scoop

Mandarin ice cream is very popular at Chinese New Year as mandarin oranges are considered traditional symbols of good fortune.

Vanilla
Ice Cream

Ingredients

- 1 tsp vanilla extract
- 20g/¾oz Silver Spoon 'Half Spoon' Sugar or Splenda Sugar Blend
- 200ml/7floz low fat crème fraiche
- 300g/9oz low fat ready-made custard

Method

- Gently combine all the ingredients together.
- Cover and leave to chill for 20-30 minutes.
- Add to the ice cream maker to churn and freeze according to your device instructions.
- Eat and enjoy immediately, or place in a container and store in the freezer.

Derived from orchids, vanilla is a much-loved flavouring: first introduced to Europe in the 1520s.

60 cals
per scoop

Gooseberry Ice Cream

Ingredients

- 200g/7oz fresh gooseberries
- 40g/1½oz Silver Spoon 'Half Spoon' Sugar or Splenda Sugar Blend
- 200ml/7floz low fat crème fraiche
- 200g/7oz low fat ready-made custard

Method

- First place the gooseberries and sugar in a saucepan with a dash of water and gently heat for 10-15 minutes, or until the gooseberries are softened and syrupy.
- Check the sweetness of the fruit and add a little more sugar if the gooseberries are still tart.
- Blend into a puree, sieve out the seeds and allow to cool for a little while.
- When cool, add the crème fraiche & custard and gently combine. Cover and leave to chill for 20-30 minutes.
- Add to the ice cream maker to churn and freeze according to your device instructions.
- Eat and enjoy immediately, or place in a container and store in the freezer.

65 cals per scoop

The amount of sugar needed may vary depending on the ripeness of the fruit so make sure you taste-test as you go along.

Bramble
Ice Cream

Ingredients

- 300g/9oz fresh blackberries
- 40g/1½oz Silver Spoon 'Half Spoon' Sugar or Splenda Sugar Blend
- 300ml/10floz low fat crème fraiche

Method

- First place the blackberries and sugar in a saucepan with a dash of water and gently heat for 10-15 minutes or until they become softened and syrupy.
- Check the sweetness of the fruit and add a little more sugar if needed.
- Blend into a puree, sieve out the seeds and allow to cool for a little while.
- When cool, add the crème fraiche and gently combine.
- Cover and leave to chill for 20-30 minutes.
- Add to the ice cream maker to churn and freeze according to your device instructions.
- Eat and enjoy immediately, or place in a container and store in the freezer.

Wild blackberry picking adds to the fun of this lovely seasonal ice cream.

70 cals
per scoop

Banana Ice Cream

Ingredients

- 2 ripe bananas, peeled
- 300ml/10floz skimmed milk
- 200ml/7floz low fat crème fraiche
- 40g/1½oz Silver Spoon 'Half Spoon' Sugar or Splenda Sugar Blend

Method

- Place all the ingredients in a food processor or blender and whizz for a few seconds.
- Cover and leave to chill for 20-30 minutes.
- Add to the ice cream maker to churn and freeze according to your device instructions.
- Eat and enjoy immediately, or place in a container and store in the freezer.

50 cals per scoop

Use very ripe bananas to make the most of the fruits' own natural sweetness.

Mango & Honey Ice Cream

Ingredients

- 2 ripe mangos, peeled & stoned
- 20g/¾oz Silver Spoon 'Half Spoon' Sugar or Splenda Sugar Blend
- 100ml/3 ½floz skimmed milk
- 300ml/10floz low fat crème fraiche
- 2 tsp runny honey

Method

- First blend the mangos into a puree.
- Add the sugar, milk, crème fraiche & honey and gently combine.
- Cover and leave to chill for 20-30 minutes.
- Add to the ice cream maker to churn and freeze according to your device instructions.
- Eat and enjoy immediately, or place in a container and store in the freezer.

There's no need to sieve the pureed mango. It's fine just as it comes.

67 cals **per scoop**

Banana & Macadamia Ice Cream

Ingredients

- 1½ ripe bananas, peeled
- 200ml/7floz skimmed milk
- 200ml/7floz low fat crème fraiche
- 50g/2oz Silver Spoon 'Half Spoon' Sugar or Splenda Sugar Blend
- 50g/2oz macadamia nuts, finely chopped

Method

- Place the bananas, milk, crème fraiche & sugar in a food processor or blender and whizz for a few seconds.
- Cover and leave to chill for 20-30 minutes.
- Add to the ice cream maker to churn and freeze according to your device instructions.
- When the ice cream has reached the desired consistency tip in the finely chopped nuts and leave to churn for a minute longer.
- Eat and enjoy immediately, or place in a container and store in the freezer.

88 cals per scoop

Macadamia nuts and bananas are a classic combination. Chop the nuts finely so that they are spread evenly throughout the finished ice cream.

Almond & Vanilla Ice Cream

Ingredients

- ¾ tsp each of vanilla & almond extracts
- 20g/¾oz Silver Spoon 'Half Spoon' Sugar or Splenda Sugar Blend
- 300ml/10floz low fat crème fraiche
- 150g/5oz low fat ready-made custard

Method

- Gently combine all the ingredients together.
- Cover and leave to chill for 20-30 minutes.
- Add to the ice cream maker to churn and freeze according to your device instructions.
- Eat and enjoy immediately, or place in a container and store in the freezer.

Almond and vanilla extracts combine delicately in this lovely ice cream. Chopped almonds make a lovely garnish too.

60 cals per scoop

Mint Choc Chip Ice Cream

Ingredients

- **50g/2oz milk chocolate, melted**
- **½ tsp peppermint extract**
- **15g/½oz Silver Spoon 'Half Spoon' Sugar or Splenda Sugar Blend**
- **250ml/8floz low fat crème fraiche**
- **200g/7oz low fat ready-made custard**
- **25g/1oz chocolate chips, very finely chopped**

Method

- Allow the melted chocolate to cool and gently combine with the peppermint, sugar, crème fraiche & custard.
- Cover and leave to chill for 20-30 minutes.
- Add to the ice cream maker to churn and freeze according to your device instructions.
- When the ice cream has reached the desired consistency, tip in the chopped chocolate chips and combine in the ice cream maker for a minute or two longer.
- Eat and enjoy immediately, or place in a container and store in the freezer.

84 cals per scoop

Add more or less peppermint extract depending on how minty you like your ice cream. You could also make a version of this ice cream using freshly chopped mint leaves in place of the peppermint extract.

28

Coffee & Creme Ice Cream

Ingredients

- 200ml/7floz light condensed milk
- 100ml/3½floz low fat crème fraiche
- 200ml/7floz skimmed milk
- 2 tbsp espresso powder

Method

- Gently combine all the ingredients together.
- Cover and leave to chill for 20-30 minutes.
- Add to the ice cream maker to churn and freeze according to your device instructions.
- Eat and enjoy immediately, or place in a container and store in the freezer.

This is grown-ups ice cream! Try a substituting one tablespoon of the espresso powder with one tablespoon of cocoa powder for a 'mocha' taste.

70 cals per scoop

Cardamom & Coconut Ice Cream

Ingredients

- **20g/¾oz Silver Spoon 'Half Spoon' Sugar or Splenda Sugar Blend**
- **300ml/10floz low fat crème fraiche**
- **150ml/5floz low fat coconut milk**
- **¼tsp each ground cardamom and cloves**

Method

- Gently combine all the ingredients together.
- Cover and leave to chill for 20-30 minutes.
- Add to the ice cream maker to churn and freeze according to your device instructions.
- Eat and enjoy immediately, or place in a container and store in the freezer.

75 cals per scoop

Cardamom is an intensely aromatic Indian spice with a coolness some consider similar to the quality of mint.

Pineapple Crush Ice Cream

Ingredients

- 200g/7oz fresh pineapple
- 40g/1½oz Silver Spoon 'Half Spoon' Sugar or Splenda Sugar Blend
- 300ml/10floz low fat crème fraiche

Method

- Use a food processor to finely chop the pineapple.
- Add the sugar & crème fraiche and gently combine.
- Cover and leave to chill for 20-30 minutes.
- Add to the ice cream maker to churn and freeze according to your device instructions.
- Eat and enjoy immediately, or place in a container and store in the freezer.

Use tinned, drained pineapple if you don't have fresh pineapple to hand.

70 cals
per scoop

Chocolate Coconut Ice Cream

Ingredients

- 1 tbsp cocoa powder
- 75ml/3floz low fat coconut milk
- 15g/½oz Silver Spoon 'Half Spoon' Sugar or Splenda Sugar Blend
- 300ml/10floz low fat crème fraiche
- 125g/4oz low fat ready-made custard

Method

- Mix the cocoa powder with a tiny amount of boiling water to make a paste & allow to cool for a few minutes.
- Gently combine all the ingredients together.
- Cover and leave to chill for 20-30 minutes.
- Add to the ice cream maker to churn and freeze according to your device instructions.
- Eat and enjoy immediately, or place in a container and store in the freezer.

76 cals per scoop

You could use coconut cream for an even richer texture but this will increase the calories.

Banana & Kiwi Ice Cream

Ingredients

- 1½ ripe bananas, peeled
- 1 ripe kiwi fruit, peeled
- 200ml/7floz skimmed milk
- 200ml/7floz low fat crème fraiche
- 50g/2oz Silver Spoon 'Half Spoon' Sugar or Splenda Sugar Blend

Method

- Place all the ingredients in a food processor or blender and whizz for a few seconds.
- Cover and leave to chill for 20-30 minutes.
- Add to the ice cream maker to churn and freeze according to your device instructions.
- Eat and enjoy immediately, or place in a container and store in the freezer.

The kiwi seeds add a nice texture to the ice cream.

70 cals
per scoop

Skinny ice cream

Chocolate & Chilli Ice Cream

Ingredients

- **50g/2oz dark chocolate, melted**
- **300ml/10floz low fat crème fraiche**
- **200g/7oz low fat ready-made custard**
- **1 tsp chilli powder**
- **1 tsp runny honey**

Method

- Allow the melted chocolate to cool for a few minutes.
- Gently combine the chocolate, crème fraiche, custard, chilli & honey together.
- Cover and leave to chill for 20-30 minutes.
- Add to the ice cream maker to churn and freeze according to your device instructions.
- Eat and enjoy immediately, or place in a container and store in the freezer.

85 cals
per scoop

Spice is a question of taste! Adjust the chilli powder to suit your own palate.

Apricot Ice Cream

Ingredients

- ½tsp each of vanilla & almond extract
- 20g/¾oz Silver Spoon 'Half Spoon' Sugar or Splenda Sugar Blend
- 200g/7oz tinned apricots, drained
- 200ml/7floz low fat crème fraiche
- 125g/4oz low fat ready-made custard

Method

- Gently combine all the ingredients together.
- Cover and leave to chill for 20-30 minutes.
- Add to the ice cream maker to churn and freeze according to your device instructions.
- Eat and enjoy immediately, or place in a container and store in the freezer.

Fresh ripe apricots are good, but tinned are much easier for a quick ice cream.

60 cals
per scoop

Stewed Rhubarb & Custard Ice Cream

Ingredients

- 200g/7oz fresh rhubarb
- 40g/1½oz Silver Spoon 'Half Spoon' Sugar or Splenda Sugar Blend
- 120ml/4floz low fat crème fraiche
- 200g/7oz low fat ready-made custard

Method

- Chop the rhubarb and place in a saucepan with the sugar.
- Gently heat and leave to stew until the rhubarb is softened and syrupy.
- Check the sweetness and add a little more sugar if the rhubarb is still tart.
- When cool, add the crème fraiche & custard and gently combine.
- Cover and leave to chill for 20-30 minutes.
- Add to the ice cream maker to churn and freeze according to your device instructions.
- Eat and enjoy immediately, or place in a container and store in the freezer.

60 cals per scoop

Balancing the sweetness of the stewed rhubarb is crucial to this ice cream.

Coconut Cream Ice

Ingredients

- 20g/¾oz Silver Spoon 'Half Spoon' Sugar or Splenda Sugar Blend
- 300ml/10floz low fat crème fraiche
- 150ml/5floz low fat coconut milk
- 1 tbsp desiccated coconut

Method

- Gently combine all the ingredients together.
- Cover and leave to chill for 20-30 minutes.
- Add to the ice cream maker to churn and freeze according to your device instructions.
- Eat and enjoy immediately, or place in a container and store in the freezer.

If you don't like the texture of desiccated coconut just leave it out of the recipe and the ice cream will be completely smooth instead.

85 cals
per scoop

Banana & Cinnamon Ice Cream

Ingredients

- 2 ripe bananas, peeled
- ½tsp ground cinnamon
- 200ml/7floz skimmed milk
- 200ml/7floz low fat crème fraiche
- 50g/2oz Silver Spoon 'Half Spoon' Sugar or Splenda Sugar Blend

Method

- Place all the ingredients in a food processor or blender and whizz for a few seconds.
- Cover and leave to chill for 20-30 minutes.
- Add to the ice cream maker to churn and freeze according to your device instructions.
- Eat and enjoy immediately, or place in a container and store in the freezer.

70 cals per scoop

This makes a lovely aromatic ice. Adjust the cinnamon to suit your own taste.

Dark Chocolate Ice Cream

Ingredients

- 75g/3oz dark chocolate, melted
- 200ml/7floz low fat crème fraiche
- 200g/7oz low fat ready-made custard

Method

- Allow the melted chocolate to cool for a few minutes.
- Gently combine the chocolate, crème fraiche & custard together.
- Cover and leave to chill for 20-30 minutes.
- Add to the ice cream maker to churn and freeze according to your device instructions.
- Eat and enjoy immediately, or place in a container and store in the freezer.

To melt the dark chocolate, first break it into small pieces and place in a glass bowl over the top of a pan of boiling water.

75 cals per scoop

Rustic Raspberry Ice Cream

Ingredients

- 400g/14oz fresh raspberries
- 40g/1½oz Silver Spoon 'Half Spoon' Sugar or Splenda Sugar Blend
- 200ml/7floz low fat crème fraiche
- 1 tsp lemon juice

Method

- Leave the raspberries whole, add the sugar, crème fraiche & lemon juice and gently combine.
- Cover and leave to chill for 20-30 minutes.
- Add to the ice cream maker to churn and freeze according to your device instructions.
- Eat and enjoy immediately, or place in a container and store in the freezer.

58 cals per scoop

Leaving the raspberries whole gives the ice cream a rustic coarse texture. Of course you can puree it if you prefer.

Candied Ginger & Banana Ice Cream

Ingredients

- 2 ripe bananas, peeled
- 200ml/7floz skimmed milk
- 200ml/7floz low fat crème fraiche
- 50g/2oz candied ginger

Method

- Place all the ingredients in a food processor or blender and whizz for a few seconds (making sure the candied ginger is finely chopped).
- Cover and leave to chill for 20-30 minutes.
- Add to the ice cream maker to churn and freeze according to your device instructions.
- Eat and enjoy immediately, or place in a container and store in the freezer.

If at the end of churning you find you want the ice cream a little sweeter add a teaspoon of runny honey and churn for a minute or two longer.

55 cals
per scoop

Hazelnut Mocha Ice Cream

Ingredients

- 1 tbsp espresso powder
- 1 tbsp cocoa powder
- 200ml/7floz light condensed milk
- 100ml/3½oz skimmed milk
- 140ml/4½floz low fat crème fraiche
- 50g/2oz hazelnuts, finely chopped

Method

- Mix the espresso & cocoa powder with a tiny amount of boiling water to make a paste and allow to cool for a few minutes.
- Gently combine all the ingredients together, except the chopped hazelnuts.
- Cover and leave to chill for 20-30 minutes.
- Add to the ice cream maker to churn and freeze according to your device instructions.
- When the ice cream has reached the desired consistency tip in the chopped hazelnuts and combine in the ice cream maker for a few seconds.
- Eat and enjoy immediately, or place in a container and store in the freezer.

95 cals per scoop

Hazelnuts taste even better if they are gently toasted in a dry frying pan for a minute or two before chopping.

Spiced Plum Ice Cream

Ingredients

- 200g/7oz ripe plums, stoned & chopped
- ¼tsp each ground all spice, cinnamon & nutmeg
- 40g/1½oz Silver Spoon 'Half Spoon' Sugar or Splenda Sugar Blend
- 140ml/4½floz low fat crème fraiche
- 200g/7oz low fat ready-made custard

Method

- First place the chopped plums, dried spices, sugar & a dash of water in a saucepan and gently heat until the plums are well stewed and steeped in the aromatic spices.
- Check the sweetness of the fruit and add a little more sugar if needed.
- Blend into a puree and allow to cool for a little while.
- When cool, add the crème fraiche & custard and gently combine.
- Cover and leave to chill for 20-30 minutes.
- Add to the ice cream maker to churn and freeze according to your device instructions.
- Eat and enjoy immediately, or place in a container and store in the freezer.

Feel free to alter the balance of spices to suit your own taste.

60 cals
per scoop

Skinny ice cream

Raisin & Vanilla Ice Cream

Ingredients

- 2 tbsp raisins
- 1 tsp vanilla extract
- 20g/¾oz Silver Spoon 'Half Spoon' Sugar or Splenda Sugar Blend
- 200ml/7floz low fat crème fraiche
- 200g/7oz low fat ready-made custard
- ¼ tsp ground nutmeg

Method

- Blitz the raisins in a food processor for a few seconds until finely chopped.
- Gently combine all the ingredients together.
- Cover and leave to chill for 20-30 minutes.
- Add to the ice cream maker to churn and freeze according to your device instructions.
- Eat and enjoy immediately, or place in a container and store in the freezer.

62 cals
per scoop

A shot of Rum is a classic addition to this ice cream flavour but it's not a necessity!

Wasabi
Ice Cream

Ingredients

- 1 tsp wasabi mustard
- 20g/¾oz Silver Spoon 'Half Spoon' Sugar or Splenda Sugar Blend
- 200ml/7floz low fat crème fraiche
- 200g/7oz low fat ready-made custard
- 1 tsp lemon juice

Method

- Gently combine all the ingredients together.
- Cover and leave to chill for 20-30 minutes.
- Add to the ice cream maker to churn and freeze according to your device instructions.
- Eat and enjoy immediately, or place in a container and store in the freezer.

Wasabi is a brightly coloured Japanese mustard widely available in most supermarkets. If you do invest in a tube you'll find lots of other culinary uses for it.

55 cals
per scoop

Lime & Cream Cheese Ice Cream

Ingredients

- 75g/3oz low fat cream cheese
- 200ml/7floz skimmed milk
- 200ml/7floz low fat crème fraiche
- 25g/1oz Silver Spoon 'Half Spoon' Sugar or Splenda Sugar Blend
- Juice of 1 lime

Method

- Gently combine all the ingredients together.
- Cover and leave to chill for 20-30 minutes.
- Add to the ice cream maker to churn and freeze according to your device instructions.
- Eat and enjoy immediately, or place in a container and store in the freezer.

55 cals per scoop

Cream cheese makes a lovely addition to ice cream recipes. Add a little honey if you feel you need to increase the sweetness.

Peanut Butter
Ice Cream

Ingredients

- 2 tbsp smooth peanut butter
- 15g/½oz Silver Spoon 'Half Spoon' Sugar or Splenda Sugar Blend
- 200ml/7floz low fat crème fraiche
- 200g/7oz low fat ready-made custard

Method

- Gently combine all the ingredients together.
- Cover and leave to chill for 20-30 minutes.
- Add to the ice cream maker to churn and freeze according to your device instructions.
- Eat and enjoy immediately, or place in a container and store in the freezer.

You could use crunchy peanut butter if you prefer but smooth seems to be the favourite.

75 cals
per scoop

Peaches & Creme Ice Cream

Ingredients

- 200g/7oz tinned peaches, drained
- 100ml/3½floz light condensed milk
- 200ml/7floz low fat crème fraiche
- 1 tsp lemon juice

Method

- Blitz the peaches in a food processor for a few seconds until they are very finely chopped.
- Gently combine all the ingredients together.
- Cover and leave to chill for 20-30 minutes.
- Add to the ice cream maker to churn and freeze according to your device instructions.
- Eat and enjoy immediately, or place in a container and store in the freezer.

85 cals per scoop

You can puree the peaches if you prefer to have a smooth evenly spread texture rather than peach pieces.

Butternut Squash Ice Cream

Ingredients

- 200g/7oz butternut squash flesh
- 15g/½oz Silver Spoon 'Half Spoon' Sugar or Splenda Sugar Blend
- 200ml/7floz low fat crème fraiche
- 200g/7oz low fat ready-made custard
- ½ tsp ground ginger

Method

- Puree the cooked butternut squash flesh.
- Gently combine all the ingredients together.
- Cover and leave to chill for 20-30 minutes.
- Add to the ice cream maker to churn and freeze according to your device instructions.
- Eat and enjoy immediately, or place in a container and store in the freezer.

To prepare the squash: peel, deseed & cut into chunks. Lightly brush with olive oil and cook in a preheated oven at 400f/200c until tender.

70 cals
per scoop

Runny Honey Ice Cream

Ingredients

- **2 tbsp runny honey**
- **200ml/7floz low fat crème fraiche**
- **200g/7oz low fat ready-made custard**

Method

- Gently combine all the ingredients together.
- Cover and leave to chill for 20-30 minutes.
- Add to the ice cream maker to churn and freeze according to your device instructions.
- Eat and enjoy immediately, or place in a container and store in the freezer.

75 cals
per scoop

Use a good quality honey for this recipe, its taste and texture will be worth it.

Citrus Zest Ice Cream

Ingredients

- Zest and juice of 2 fresh oranges
- 200ml/7floz light condensed milk
- 200ml/7floz low fat crème fraiche
- 100ml/3½floz skimmed milk

Method

- Gently combine all the ingredients together.
- Cover and leave to chill for 20-30 minutes.
- Add to the ice cream maker to churn and freeze according to your device instructions.
- Eat and enjoy immediately, or place in a container and store in the freezer.

Reserve a little of the zest to sprinkle over the ice cream when serving.

90 cals
per scoop

Smooth Avocado Ice Cream

Ingredients

- 1 ripe avocado, peeled & stoned
- 200ml/7floz skimmed milk
- 200ml/7floz low fat crème fraiche
- 50g/2oz Silver Spoon 'Half Spoon' Sugar or Splenda Sugar Blend

Method

- Place all the ingredients in a food processor or blender and whizz for a few seconds until the avocado is pureed.
- Cover and leave to chill for 20-30 minutes.
- Add to the ice cream maker to churn and freeze according to your device instructions.
- Eat and enjoy immediately, or place in a container and store in the freezer.

70 cals per scoop

Avocados have a naturally smooth and creamy texture, which is perfect for ice cream making.

Fresh Basil
Ice Cream

Ingredients

- 2 tbsp freshly chopped basil leaves
- 15g/½oz Silver Spoon 'Half Spoon' Sugar or Splenda Sugar Blend
- 200ml/7floz low fat crème fraiche
- 200g/7oz low fat ready-made custard

Method

- Gently combine all the ingredients together.
- Cover and leave to chill for 20-30 minutes.
- Add to the ice cream maker to churn and freeze according to your device instructions.
- Eat and enjoy immediately, or place in a container and store in the freezer.

Basil may sound like an odd flavour for ice cream but it has a lovely subtle sweetness. Ensure it is very finely chopped so that tiny flecks are spread evenly throughout the mixture.

55 cals
per scoop

Blueberry & Coconut Cream Ice

Ingredients

- 250g/9oz blueberries
- 20g/¾oz Silver Spoon 'Half Spoon' Sugar or Splenda Sugar Blend
- 200ml/7floz low fat crème fraiche
- 150ml/5floz low fat coconut milk

Method

- First puree the blueberries.
- Gently combine all the ingredients together.
- Cover and leave to chill for 20-30 minutes.
- Add to the ice cream maker to churn and freeze according to your device instructions.
- Eat and enjoy immediately, or place in a container and store in the freezer.

65 cals
per scoop

You could also try adding a little lime to this recipe for a different twist.

Mascarpone Cheese Ice Cream

Ingredients

- ½tsp vanilla essence
- 75g/3oz low fat mascarpone cheese
- 200ml/7floz skimmed milk
- 200ml/7floz low fat crème fraiche
- 50g/2oz Silver Spoon 'Half Spoon' Sugar or Splenda Sugar Blend

Method

- Gently combine all the ingredients together.
- Cover and leave to chill for 20-30 minutes.
- Add to the ice cream maker to churn and freeze according to your device instructions.
- Eat and enjoy immediately, or place in a container and store in the freezer.

Mascarpone cheese is a surprisingly popular ingredient in Italian ice cream making.

90 cals per scoop

Fig Ice Cream

Ingredients

- **75g/3oz dried figs**
- **15g/½oz Silver Spoon 'Half Spoon' Sugar or Splenda Sugar Blend**
- **200ml/7floz low fat crème fraiche**
- **200g/7oz low fat ready-made custard**

Method

- Place the figs in a saucepan with a little water. Bring to the boil and poach for a few minutes.
- Puree the stewed figs with 2 tbsp of the poaching liquid and allow to cool.
- Gently combine all the ingredients together.
- Cover and leave to chill for 20-30 minutes.
- Add to the ice cream maker to churn and freeze according to your device instructions.
- Eat and enjoy immediately, or place in a container and store in the freezer.

75 cals per scoop

A little lemon zest makes a good addition to this recipe.

Saffron & Nutmeg Ice Cream

Ingredients

- 1 tsp saffron threads
- ½ tsp ground nutmeg
- 15g/½oz Silver Spoon 'Half Spoon' Sugar or Splenda Sugar Blend
- 200ml/7floz low fat crème fraiche
- 200g/7oz low fat ready-made custard

Method

- Gently combine all the ingredients together.
- Cover and leave to chill for 20-30 minutes.
- Add to the ice cream maker to churn and freeze according to your device instructions.
- Eat and enjoy immediately, or place in a container and store in the freezer.

Try serving this ice cream with some freshly chopped pistachio nuts…. delicious!

55 cals
per scoop

Honey & Lemon Ice Cream

Ingredients

- 200ml/7floz light condensed milk
- 200ml/7floz low fat crème fraiche
- Juice and zest of 1 lemon
- 2 tbsp runny honey

Method

- Gently combine all the ingredients together.
- Cover and leave to chill for 20-30 minutes.
- Add to the ice cream maker to churn and freeze according to your device instructions.
- Eat and enjoy immediately, or place in a container and store in the freezer.

90 cals
per scoop

Reserve a little of the lemon zest to serve as a garnish if you wish.

Mango
Ice Cream

Ingredients

- 2 ripe mangos, peeled & stoned
- 40g/1½oz Silver Spoon 'Half Spoon' Sugar or Splenda Sugar Blend
- 300ml/10floz low fat crème fraiche
- 1 tbsp lemon juice

Method

- First blend the mangos into a puree.
- Add the sugar, crème fraiche & lemon juice and gently combine.
- Cover and leave to chill for 20-30 minutes.
- Add to the ice cream maker to churn and freeze according to your device instructions.
- Eat and enjoy immediately, or place in a container and store in the freezer.

Make sure the mangos are very ripe and sweet.

80 cals
per scoop

Apple Juice Ice Cream

Ingredients

- 120ml/4floz apple juice
- 100ml/3 ½floz light condensed milk
- 300ml/10floz low fat crème fraiche
- 2 tbsp lemon juice

Method

- Gently combine all the ingredients together.
- Cover and leave to chill for 20-30 minutes.
- Add to the ice cream maker to churn and freeze according to your device instructions.
- Eat and enjoy immediately, or place in a container and store in the freezer.

70 cals
per scoop

This is not a particularly creamy ice cream but it's super-light and fresh tasting.

THE Skinny ICE CREAM MAKER

Skinny frozen yogurt

Remember if freezing, remove from the freezer approx. 10-15 minutes before serving or to the refrigerator for approx. 30-35 minutes to get the best serving texture.

Honey Peach Frozen Yogurt

Ingredients

- **200g/7oz tinned peaches, drained**
- **2 tsp runny honey**
- **400g/14oz low fat natural yogurt**

Method

- Place the peaches in a blender and puree.
- Gently combine the peach puree, honey and yogurt.
- Cover and leave to chill for 20-30 minutes.
- Add to the ice cream maker to churn and freeze according to your device instructions.
- Eat and enjoy immediately, or place in a container and store in the freezer.

40 cals
per scoop

Tinned peaches make a for super-quick recipe which you can enjoy in 15 minutes from start to finish.

Banana Frozen Yogurt

Ingredients

- **2 ripe bananas**
- **400g/14oz low fat natural yogurt**
- **50g/2oz Silver Spoon 'Half Spoon' Sugar or Splenda Sugar Blend**

Method

- Place the bananas in a blender and puree.
- Gently combine the banana puree, yogurt & sugar.
- Cover and leave to chill for 20-30 minutes.
- Add to the ice cream maker to churn and freeze according to your device instructions.
- Eat and enjoy immediately, or place in a container and store in the freezer.

Use very ripe bananas for this recipe as they will be bursting with natural sugars.

60 cals per scoop

Skinny frozen yogurt

Strawberry Frozen Yogurt

Ingredients

- **200g/7oz fresh strawberries**
- **400g/14oz low fat natural yogurt**
- **40g/1½oz Silver Spoon 'Half Spoon' Sugar or Splenda Sugar Blend**

Method

- Place the strawberries in a blender and puree.
- Gently combine the strawberry puree, yogurt & sugar.
- Cover and leave to chill for 20-30 minutes.
- Add to the ice cream maker to churn and freeze according to your device instructions.
- Eat and enjoy immediately, or place in a container and store in the freezer.

45 cals per scoop

If you prefer not to have seeds in your yogurt, pass the strawberry puree through a sieve.

Raspberry & Honey Frozen Yogurt

Ingredients

- 200g/11oz fresh raspberries
- 400g/14oz low fat natural yogurt
- 1½ tbsp runny honey

Method

- Place the raspberries in a blender and puree.
- Sieve out the seeds and gently combine with the yogurt and honey.
- Cover and leave to chill for 20-30 minutes.
- Add to the ice cream maker to churn and freeze according to your device instructions.
- Eat and enjoy immediately, or place in a container and store in the freezer.

Adjust the quantity of honey to suit your own taste.

50 cals
per scoop

Espresso
Frozen Yogurt

Ingredients

- **1 tbsp espresso powder**
- **500g/1lb 2oz low fat natural yogurt**
- **40g/1½oz Silver Spoon 'Half Spoon' Sugar or Splenda Sugar Blend**

Method

- Gently combine all the ingredients together.
- Cover and leave to chill for 20-30 minutes.
- Add to the ice cream maker to churn and freeze according to your device instructions.
- Eat and enjoy immediately, or place in a container and store in the freezer.

55 cals
per scoop

You may want to experiment with the coffee quantity in this yogurt depending on the variety of espresso you use.

Maple Syrup Frozen Yogurt

Ingredients

- 1 tbsp maple syrup
- 100ml/3½oz skimmed condensed milk
- 400g/14oz low fat natural yogurt

Method

- Gently combine all the ingredients together.
- Cover and leave to chill for 20-30 minutes.
- Add to the ice cream maker to churn and freeze according to your device instructions.
- Eat and enjoy immediately, or place in a container and store in the freezer.

Maple syrup and condensed milk make for a lovely rich yogurt.

65 cals per scoop

Balsamic Strawberry Frozen Yogurt

Ingredients

- 200g/7oz fresh strawberries
- 300g/11oz low fat natural yogurt
- 100ml/3½floz skimmed condensed milk
- 2 tbsp balsamic vinegar
- ½ tsp vanilla essence

Method

- Place the strawberries into a blender and puree.
- Pass through and sieve and combine with the other ingredients.
- Cover and leave to chill for 20-30 minutes.
- Add to the ice cream maker to churn and freeze according to your device instructions.
- Eat and enjoy immediately, or place in a container and store in the freezer.

60 cals per scoop

Vanilla and balsamic make a great combination. If your strawberries are not very ripe you may need to add a little sugar.

Chocolate Frozen Yogurt

Ingredients

- 50g/2oz milk chocolate, melted
- 500g/1lb 2oz low fat natural yogurt
- 40g/1oz Silver Spoon 'Half Spoon' Sugar or Splenda Sugar Blend

Method

- Allow the melted chocolate to cool.
- Gently combine all the ingredients together.
- Cover and leave to chill for 20-30 minutes.
- Add to the ice cream maker to churn and freeze according to your device instructions.
- Eat and enjoy immediately, or place in a container and store in the freezer.

Good quality chocolate makes for a better tasting frozen yogurt.

70 cals
per scoop

Pomegranate Juice Frozen Yogurt

Ingredients

- 200ml/7floz pomegranate juice
- 400g/14oz low fat natural yogurt
- 25g/1oz Silver Spoon 'Half Spoon' Sugar or Splenda Sugar Blend

Method

- Gently combine all the ingredients.
- Cover and leave to chill for 20-30 minutes.
- Add to the ice cream maker to churn and freeze according to your device instructions.
- Eat and enjoy immediately, or place in a container and store in the freezer.

45 cals per scoop

A garnish of fresh pomegranate seeds makes a lovely addition to this fro-yo!

Kiwi
Frozen Yogurt

Ingredients

- **3 ripe kiwis, peeled**
- **500g/1lb 2oz low fat natural yogurt**
- **40g/1½oz Silver Spoon 'Half Spoon' Sugar or Splenda Sugar Blend**

Method

- Place the kiwis in a blender and puree.
- Gently combine the kiwi puree with the yogurt & sugar
- Cover and leave to chill for 20-30 minutes.
- Add to the ice cream maker to churn and freeze according to your device instructions.
- Eat and enjoy immediately, or place in a container and store in the freezer.

This recipe is lovely served in the morning over fresh granola.

55 cals
per scoop

Coconut Cream Frozen Yogurt

Skinny frozen yogurt

Ingredients

- **2 tbsp coconut cream**
- **500g/1lb 2oz low fat natural yogurt**
- **25g/1oz Silver Spoon 'Half Spoon' Sugar or Splenda Sugar Blend**

Method

- Gently combine all the ingredients together.
- Cover and leave to chill for 20-30 minutes.
- Add to the ice cream maker to churn and freeze according to your device instructions.
- Eat and enjoy immediately, or place in a container and store in the freezer.

60 cals per scoop

Add a little desiccated coconut to this recipe if you want to introduce a coarse texture.

Mint
Frozen Yogurt

Ingredients

- 400g/14oz low fat natural yogurt
- 100ml/3½oz skimmed condensed milk
- 50g/2oz fresh mint leaves

Method

- Chop the mint leaves very finely and combine with the other ingredients.
- Cover and leave to chill for 20-30 minutes.
- Add to the ice cream maker to churn and freeze according to your device instructions.
- Eat and enjoy immediately, or place in a container and store in the freezer.

Fresh mint is great with yogurt. You could also use peppermint essence as an alternative.

52 cals
per scoop

Almond & Pistachio Frozen Yogurt

Ingredients

- 1 tsp almond extract
- 500g/1lb 2oz low fat natural yogurt
- 50g/2oz Silver Spoon 'Half Spoon' Sugar or Splenda Sugar Blend
- 50g/2oz chopped pistachio nut

Method

- Gently combine together the almond extract, yogurt and sugar.
- Cover and leave to chill for 20-30 minutes.
- Add to the ice cream maker to churn and freeze according to your device instructions.
- When the texture looks ready tip in the chopped pistachios and churn for a minute longer.
- Eat and enjoy immediately, or place in a container and store in the freezer.

65 cals per scoop

Pistachio nuts are closely related to cashews; which you can easily substitute in this recipe.

Vanilla & Blueberry Frozen Yogurt

Ingredients

- 200g/11oz fresh blueberries
- 50g/2oz Silver Spoon 'Half Spoon' Sugar or Splenda Sugar Blend
- 400g/14oz low fat natural yogurt
- 1 tsp vanilla extract

Method

- Gently stew the blueberries and sugar with a dash of water in a saucepan on a gentle heat for 10-15 minutes or until they become syrupy and pulped.
- Place the stewed blueberries in a blender. Puree and leave to cool.
- Gently combine with the yogurt & vanilla extract.
- Cover and leave to chill for 20-30 minutes.
- Add to the ice cream maker to churn and freeze according to your device instructions.
- Eat and enjoy immediately, or place in a container and store in the freezer.

This recipe will make a smooth yogurt. Don't blend the blueberries if you want a chunkier texture.

48 cals
per scoop

Berry Banana Frozen Yogurt

Ingredients

- 1 ripe banana
- 200g/7oz fresh strawberries
- 300g/11oz low fat natural yogurt
- 40g/1½oz Silver Spoon 'Half Spoon' Sugar or Splenda Sugar Blend
- 1 tsp lemon juice

Method

- Place all the ingredients into a blender and puree.
- Cover and leave to chill for 20-30 minutes.
- Add to the ice cream maker to churn and freeze according to your device instructions.
- Eat and enjoy immediately, or place in a container and store in the freezer.

40 cals per scoop

Adjust the sugar depending on the ripeness of your fruit, you may need less!

Nutella
Frozen Yogurt

Ingredients

- **2 tbsp nutella or other chocolate hazelnut spread**
- **500g/1lb 2oz low fat natural yogurt**
- **7g/¼oz Silver Spoon 'Half Spoon' Sugar or Splenda Sugar Blend**

Method

- Gently combine the ingredients together.
- Cover and leave to chill for 20-30 minutes.
- Add to the ice cream maker to churn and freeze according to your device instructions.
- Eat and enjoy immediately, or place in a container and store in the freezer.

This frozen yogurt is great served with fresh strawberries.

45 cals
per scoop

Peanut Butter Fro-Yo

Ingredients

- **2 tbsp smooth low fat peanut butter**
- **400g/14oz low fat natural yogurt**
- **100ml/3½floz skimmed condensed milk**

Method

- Gently combine the ingredients together.
- Cover and leave to chill for 20-30 minutes.
- Add to the ice cream maker to churn and freeze according to your device instructions.
- Eat and enjoy immediately, or place in a container and store in the freezer.

70 cals per scoop

Use crunchy peanut butter if you prefer its texture.

THE Skinny ICE CREAM MAKER

Skinny sorbet

Helpful Tips

Remember if you are freezing your sorbet, remove from the freezer approx. 10-15 minutes before serving or to the refrigerator for approx. 30-35 minutes to get the best serving texture.

Pineapple Sorbet

Ingredients

- **200ml/7floz pineapple juice**
- **100ml/3½floz water**
- **25g/1oz Silver Spoon 'Half Spoon' Sugar or Splenda Sugar Blend**
- **200g/7oz tinned pineapple**
- **1 tsp lemon juice**

Method

- Gently bring the juice, water and sugar to the boil in a saucepan for five minutes or until the sugar has dissolved. (Don't stir during this process).
- Put to one side to cool.
- Place all the ingredients into a blender and puree.
- Cover and leave to chill for 20-30 minutes.
- Add to the ice cream maker to churn and freeze according to your device instructions.
- Eat and enjoy immediately, or place in a container and store in the freezer.

40 cals per scoop

This light sorbet also works well with mango as the main ingredient.

Fresh Raspberry Sorbet

Ingredients

- 300ml/10floz water
- 25g/1oz Silver Spoon 'Half Spoon' Sugar or Splenda Sugar Blend
- 200g/7oz fresh raspberries
- 1 tsp lemon juice

Method

- Gently bring the water and sugar to the boil in a saucepan for five minutes or until the sugar has dissolved. (Don't stir during this process).
- Put to one side to cool.
- Place all the ingredients into a blender and puree.
- Cover and leave to chill for 20-30 minutes.
- Add to the ice cream maker to churn and freeze according to your device instructions.
- Eat and enjoy immediately, or place in a container and store in the freezer.

The raspberry seeds add a crunchy texture to this lovely sorbet.

30 cals
per scoop

Summer Berry Sorbet

Skinny sorbet

Ingredients

- **300ml/10floz water**
- **25g/1oz Silver Spoon 'Half Spoon' Sugar or Splenda Sugar Blend**
- **200g/7oz mixed summer berries**
- **1 tsp lemon juice**

Method

- Gently bring the water and sugar to the boil in a saucepan for five minutes or until the sugar has dissolved. (Don't stir during this process).
- Put to one side to cool.
- Place all the ingredients into a blender and puree.
- Cover and leave to chill for 20-30 minutes.
- Add to the ice cream maker to churn and freeze according to your device instructions.
- Eat and enjoy immediately, or place in a container and store in the freezer.

20 cals per scoop

Any mixture of soft fruit berries work well for this recipe.

Apricot Sorbet

Ingredients

- 200ml/7floz apricot juice
- 300ml/10floz water
- 25g/1oz Silver Spoon 'Half Spoon' Sugar or Splenda Sugar Blend

Method

- Gently bring the juice, water and sugar to the boil in a saucepan for five minutes or until the sugar has dissolved. (Don't stir during this process).
- Put to one side to cool.
- Cover and leave to chill for 20-30 minutes.
- Add to the ice cream maker to churn and freeze according to your device instructions.
- Eat and enjoy immediately, or place in a container and store in the freezer.

Peach juice also works well for this sorbet.

20 cals
per scoop

Lemon Sorbet

Ingredients

- 450ml/15floz water
- 75g/3oz Silver Spoon 'Half Spoon' Sugar or Splenda Sugar Blend
- Zest & juice of 2 lemons or 6 tbsp lemon juice

Method

- Gently bring the water, sugar & lemon zest (if using) to the boil in a saucepan for five minutes or until the sugar has dissolved. (Don't stir during this process).
- Put to one side to cool.
- Strain the liquid to remove the zest and then add the lemon juice.
- Cover and leave to chill for 20-30 minutes.
- Add to the ice cream maker to churn and freeze according to your device instructions.
- Eat and enjoy immediately, or place in a container and store in the freezer.

40 cals per scoop

Garnish with a little lemon zest for extra citrus zing!

Red Currant Sorbet

Ingredients

- 300ml/10floz water
- 25g/1oz Silver Spoon 'Half Spoon' Sugar or Splenda Sugar Blend
- 200g/7oz red currants
- 100ml/3½floz fresh orange juice

Method

- Gently heat the water, sugar and red currants in a saucepan for 10-15 minutes or until the red currants are pulpy and syrupy.
- Put to one side to cool.
- Place in a blender and puree.
- Sieve out any seeds or stalks and add the orange juice.
- Cover and leave to chill for 20-30 minutes.
- Add to the ice cream maker to churn and freeze according to your device instructions.
- Eat and enjoy immediately, or place in a container and store in the freezer.

Don't worry about removing the red currant stalks as these will be sieved out after blending.

27 cals per scoop

Orange & Lime Sorbet

Ingredients

- **300ml/9floz water**
- **200ml/7floz lime & orange juice**
- **25g/1oz Silver Spoon 'Half Spoon' Sugar or Splenda Sugar Blend**
- **2 tbsp lemon juice**

Method

- Gently bring the water, lime or orange juice and sugar to the boil in a saucepan for five minutes or until the sugar has dissolved. (Don't stir during this process).
- Put to one side to cool and add the lemon juice.
- Cover and leave to chill for 20-30 minutes.
- Add to the ice cream maker to churn and freeze according to your device instructions.
- Eat and enjoy immediately, or place in a container and store in the freezer.

25 cals per scoop

This is a tangy sorbet. Increase the sugar a little if you wish.

Cranberry & Orange Sorbet

Ingredients

- 200ml/7floz water
- 40g/1½oz Silver Spoon 'Half Spoon' Sugar or Splenda Sugar Blend
- 200g/7oz cranberries
- 100ml/3½floz fresh orange juice

Method

- Gently heat the water, sugar and cranberries in a saucepan for few minutes until the red cranberries are pulpy and syrupy.
- Put to one side to cool, sieve out the seeds and add the fresh orange juice.
- Cover and leave to chill for 20-30 minutes.
- Add to the ice cream maker to churn and freeze according to your device instructions.
- Eat and enjoy immediately, or place in a container and store in the freezer.

Check the balance of sweetness in the sorbet and adjust to suit your own taste.

35 cals
per scoop

Apple Juice Sorbet

Ingredients

- 300ml/10floz apple juice
- 200ml/7floz water
- 25g/1oz Silver Spoon 'Half Spoon' Sugar or Splenda Sugar Blend
- 1 tbsp lemon juice

Method

- Gently bring the apple juice, water and sugar to the boil in a saucepan for five minutes or until the sugar has dissolved. (Don't stir during this process).
- Put to one side to cool and add the lemon juice.
- Cover and leave to chill for 20-30 minutes.
- Add to the ice cream maker to churn and freeze according to your device instructions.
- Eat and enjoy immediately, or place in a container and store in the freezer.

30 cals per scoop

After freezing, sorbets are best left to slightly thaw at room temperature for a few minutes before eating.

Cantaloupe Sorbet

Ingredients

- 200ml/7floz water
- 25g/1oz Silver Spoon 'Half Spoon' Sugar or Splenda Sugar Blend
- 1 cantaloupe melon, flesh scooped out & deseeded
- 1 tbsp lemon juice

Method

- Gently bring the water and sugar to the boil in a saucepan for five minutes or until the sugar has dissolved. (Don't stir during this process).
- Put to one side to cool.
- Place all the ingredients into a blender and puree.
- Cover and leave to chill for 20-30 minutes.
- Add to the ice cream maker to churn and freeze according to your device instructions.
- Eat and enjoy immediately, or place in a container and store in the freezer.

You can substitute cantaloupe for honeydew melon if you prefer.

25 cals
per scoop

Basil Sorbet

Ingredients

- 400ml/14floz water
- 50g/2oz Silver Spoon 'Half Spoon' Sugar or Splenda Sugar Blend
- 125g/4oz fresh basil leaves
- 2 tbsp lemon juice

Method

- Gently bring the water, sugar & basil to the boil in a saucepan for five minutes or until the sugar has dissolved. (Don't stir during this process).
- Put to one side to cool, sieve out the leaves and add the lemon juice.
- Cover and leave to chill for 20-30 minutes.
-
- Add to the ice cream maker to churn and freeze according to your device instructions.
-
- Eat and enjoy immediately, or place in a container and store in the freezer.

20 cals
per scoop

There is a minty quality to this fresh sorbet. Garnish with basil leaves if you like.

Beetroot Sorbet

Ingredients

- 200ml/7floz water
- 300ml/10floz beetroot juice
- 50g/2oz Silver Spoon 'Half Spoon' Sugar or Splenda Sugar Blend
- 2 tbsp lemon juice

Method

- Gently bring the juice, water and sugar to the boil in a saucepan for five minutes or until the sugar has dissolved. (Don't stir during this process).
- Cover and leave to chill for 20-30 minutes.
- Add to the ice cream maker to churn and freeze according to your device instructions.
- Eat and enjoy immediately, or place in a container and store in the freezer.

Beetroot juice makes for a vibrantly coloured sorbet. Add a little more lemon juice if needed.

35 cals
per scoop

Peach Sorbet

Skinny sorbet

Ingredients

- 300ml/11floz water
- 25g/1oz Silver Spoon 'Half Spoon' Sugar or Splenda Sugar Blend
- 200g/7oz tinned peaches, drained

Method

- Gently bring the water and sugar to the boil in a saucepan for five minutes or until the sugar has dissolved. (Don't stir during this process).
- Put to one side to cool.
- Place all the ingredients into a blender and puree.
- Cover and leave to chill for 20-30 minutes.
- Add to the ice cream maker to churn and freeze according to your device instructions.
- Eat and enjoy immediately, or place in a container and store in the freezer.

40 cals
per scoop

You could use a little peach or apricot jam in place of the sugar if you wish.

Yogurt Sorbet

Ingredients

- 100ml/3½floz water
- 40g/1½oz Silver Spoon 'Half Spoon' Sugar or Splenda Sugar Blend
- 400g/14oz low fat yogurt

Method

- Gently bring the water & sugar to the boil in a saucepan for five minutes or until the sugar has dissolved. (Don't stir during this process).
- Put to one side to cool.
- Combine the yogurt with the sugar and water.
- Cover and leave to chill for 20-30 minutes.
- Add to the ice cream maker to churn and freeze according to your device instructions.
- Eat and enjoy immediately, or place in a container and store in the freezer.

Use a good quality, thick natural yogurt for this simple sorbet.

55 cals
per scoop

Pear Sorbet

Ingredients

- **200ml/7floz water**
- **25g/1oz Silver Spoon 'Half Spoon' Sugar or Splenda Sugar Blend**
- **4 ripe pears, cored, peeled & chopped**

Method

- Gently heat the water, sugar and pears in a saucepan for 10-15 minutes or until the pears become pulpy and syrupy.
- Put to one side to cool.
- Place into a blender and puree.
- Cover and leave to chill for 20-30 minutes.
- Add to the ice cream maker to churn and freeze according to your device instructions.
- Eat and enjoy immediately, or place in a container and store in the freezer.

25 cals per scoop

Use tinned pears for this if you prefer, they will still benefit from stewing in the water and sugar, so just follow the method above.

Conversion Chart
Weights for dry ingredients:

Metric	Imperial
7g	¼ oz
15g	½ oz
20g	¾ oz
25g	1 oz
40g	1½oz
50g	2oz
60g	2½oz
75g	3oz
100g	3½oz
125g	4oz
140g	4½oz
150g	5oz
165g	5½oz
175g	6oz
200g	7oz
225g	8oz
250g	9oz
275g	10oz
300g	11oz
350g	12oz
375g	13oz
400g	14oz
425g	15oz
450g	1lb
500g	1lb 2oz
550g	1¼lb
600g	1lb 5oz
650g	1lb 7oz
675g	1½lb
700g	1lb 9oz
750g	1lb 11oz
800g	1¾lb
900g	2lb
1kg	2¼lb
1.1kg	2½lb
1.25kg	2¾lb
1.35kg	3lb
1.5kg	3lb 6oz
1.8kg	4lb
2kg	4½lb
2.25kg	5lb
2.5kg	5½lb
2.75kg	6lb

Conversion Chart

Liquid measures:

Metric	Imperial	Aus	US
25ml	1fl oz		
60ml	2fl oz	¼ cup	¼ cup
75ml	3fl oz		
100ml	3½fl oz		
120ml	4fl oz	½ cup	½ cup
150ml	5fl oz		
175ml	6fl oz	¾ cup	¾ cup
200ml	7fl oz		
250ml	8fl oz	1 cup	1 cup
300ml	10fl oz/½ pt	1¼ cups	
360ml	12fl oz		
400ml	14fl oz		
450ml	15fl oz	2 cups	2 cups/1 pint
600ml	1 pint	1 pint	2½ cups
750ml	1¼ pint		
900ml	1½ pints		
1 litre	1½ pints	1¾ pints	1 quart

Other CookNation Titles

You may also be interested in other titles in the CookNation series. In particular, our popular series of slow cooker titles:

You can find all the following great titles by searching under '**CookNation**'.

Review

If you enjoyed '**The Skinny Ice Cream Maker**' we'd really appreciate your feedback. Reviews help others decide if this is the right book for them so a moment of your time would be appreciated. Thank you.

The Skinny Slow Cooker Recipe Book

Delicious Recipes Under 300, 400 And 500 Calories.

Paperback / eBook

More Skinny Slow Cooker Recipes

75 More Delicious Recipes Under 300, 400 & 500 Calories.

Paperback / eBook

The Skinny Slow Cooker Curry Recipe Book

Delicious & Simple Low Calorie Curries From Around The World Under 200, 300 & 400 Calories. Perfect For Your Fast Days.

Paperback / eBook

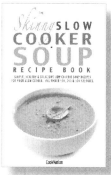

The Skinny Slow Cooker Soup Recipe Book

Simple, Healthy & Delicious Low Calorie Soup Recipes For Your Slow Cooker. All Under 100, 200 & 300 Calories.

Paperback / eBook

The Skinny Slow Cooker Vegetarian Recipe Book

40 Delicious Recipes Under 200, 300 And 400 Calories.

Paperback / eBook

The Skinny 5:2 Slow Cooker Recipe Book

Skinny Slow Cooker Recipe And Menu Ideas Under 100, 200, 300 & 400 Calories For Your 5:2 Diet.

Paperback / eBook

The Skinny 5:2 Curry Recipe Book

Spice Up Your Fast Days With Simple Low Calorie Curries, Snacks, Soups, Salads & Sides Under 200, 300 & 400 Calories

Paperback / eBook

The Skinny Halogen Oven Family Favourites Recipe Book

Healthy, Low Calorie Family Meal-Time Halogen Oven Recipes Under 300, 400 and 500 Calories

Paperback / eBook

Skinny Halogen Oven Cooking For One
Single Serving, Healthy, Low Calorie Halogen Oven Recipes Under 200, 300 and 400 Calories

Paperback / eBook

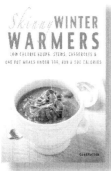

Skinny Winter Warmers Recipe Book
Soups, Stews, Casseroles & One Pot Meals Under 300, 400 & 500 Calories.

Paperback / eBook

The Skinny Soup Maker Recipe Book
Delicious Low Calorie, Healthy and Simple Soup Recipes Under 100, 200 and 300 Calories. Perfect For Any Diet and Weight Loss Plan.
Paperback / eBook

The Skinny Bread Machine Recipe Book
70 Simple, Lower Calorie, Healthy Breads...Baked To Perfection In Your Bread Maker.

Paperback / eBook

The Skinny Indian Takeaway Recipe Book

Authentic British Indian Restaurant Dishes Under 300, 400 And 500 Calories. The Secret To Low Calorie Indian Takeaway Food At Home

Paperback / eBook

The Skinny Juice Diet Recipe Book

5lbs, 5 Days. The Ultimate Kick-Start Diet and Detox Plan to Lose Weight & Feel Great!

Paperback / eBook

The Skinny 5:2 Diet Recipe Book Collection

All The 5:2 Fast Diet Recipes You'll Ever Need. All Under 100, 200, 300, 400 And 500 Calories

eBook

Available only on eBook

The Skinny 5:2 Fast Diet Meals For One

Single Serving Fast Day Recipes & Snacks Under 100, 200 & 300 Calories

Paperback / eBook

The Skinny 5:2 Fast Diet Vegetarian Meals For One

Single Serving Fast Day Recipes & Snacks Under 100, 200 & 300 Calories

Paperback / eBook

The Skinny 5:2 Fast Diet Family Favourites Recipe Book

Eat With All The Family On Your Diet Fasting Days

Paperback / eBook

The Skinny 5:2 Fast Diet Family Favorites Recipe Book *U.S.A. EDITION*

Dine With All The Family On Your Diet Fasting Days

Paperback / eBook

The Skinny 5:2 Diet Chicken Dishes Recipe Book

Delicious Low Calorie Chicken Dishes Under 300, 400 & 500 Calories

Paperback / eBook

The Skinny 5:2 Bikini Diet Recipe Book

Recipes & Meal Planners Under 100, 200 & 300 Calories. Get Ready For Summer & Lose Weight...FAST!

Paperback / eBook

The Paleo Diet For Beginners Slow Cooker Recipe Book

Gluten Free, Everyday Essential Slow Cooker Paleo Recipes For Beginners

eBook

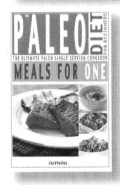

The Paleo Diet For Beginners Meals For One

The Ultimate Paleo Single Serving Cookbook

Paperback / eBook

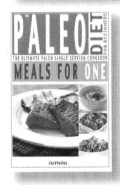

The Paleo Diet For Beginners Holidays

Thanksgiving, Christmas & New Year Paleo Friendly Recipes

eBook

The Healthy Kids Smoothie Book

40 Delicious Goodness In A Glass Recipes for Happy Kids.

eBook

The Skinny Slow Cooker Summer Recipe Book

Fresh & Seasonal Summer Recipes For Your Slow Cooker. All Under 300, 400 And 500 Calories.

Paperback / eBook

The Skinny ActiFry Cookbook

Guilt-free and Delicious ActiFry Recipe Ideas: Discover The Healthier Way to Fry!

Paperback / eBook

The Skinny 15 Minute Meals Recipe Book

Delicious, Nutritious & Super-Fast Meals in 15 Minutes Or Less. All Under 300, 400 & 500 Calories.

Paperback / eBook

The Skinny Mediterranean Recipe Book

Simple, Healthy & Delicious Low Calorie Mediterranean Diet Dishes. All Under 200, 300 & 400 Calories.

Paperback / eBook

The Skinny Hot Air Fryer Cookbook

Delicious & Simple Meals For Your Hot Air Fryer: Discover The Healthier Way To Fry.

Paperback / eBook

21508965R00061

Printed in Great Britain
by Amazon